5988 6134

ENVIRONMENTAL SCIENCE

SCIENCE 24/7

ANIMAL SCIENCE

CAR SCIENCE

COMPUTER SCIENCE

ENVIRONMENTAL SCIENCE

FASHION SCIENCE

FOOD SCIENCE

HEALTH SCIENCE

MUSIC SCIENCE

PHOTO SCIENCE

SPORTS SCIENCE

TRAVEL SCIENCE

SCIENCE 24/7

ENVIRONMENTAL SCIENCE

JANE P. GARDNER

SCIENCE CONSULTANT:
RUSS LEWIN
SCIENCE AND MATH EDUCATOR

Mason Crest

Mason Crest
450 Parkway Drive, Suite D
Broomall, PA 19008
www.masoncrest.com

© 2016 by Mason Crest, an imprint of National Highlights, Inc.

Printed and bound in the United States of America.

Series ISBN: 978-1-4222-3404-4
Hardback ISBN: 978-1-4222-3408-2
EBook ISBN: 978-1-4222-8492-6

First printing
1 3 5 7 9 8 6 4 2

Produced by Shoreline Publishing Group LLC
Santa Barbara, California
Editorial Director: James Buckley Jr.
Designer: Patty Kelley
www.shorelinepublishing.com
Cover Image from Dollar Photo Club.

Library of Congress Cataloging-in-Publication Data on file with the Publisher.

IMPORTANT NOTICE
The science experiments, activities, and information described in this publication are for educational use only. The publisher is not responsible for any direct, indirect, incidental or consequential damages as a result of the uses or misuses of the techniques and information within.

Contents

KEY ICONS TO LOOK FOR

Words to Understand: These words with their easy-to-understand definitions will increase the reader's understanding of the text, while building vocabulary skills.

Sidebars: This boxed material within the main text allows readers to build knowledge, gain insights, explore possibilities, and broaden their perspectives by weaving together additional information to provide realistic and holistic perspectives.

Series Glossary of Key Terms: This back-of-the-book glossary contains terminology used throughout this series. Words found here increase the reader's ability to read and comprehend higher-level books and articles in this field.

INTRODUCTION

Science. Ugh! Is this the class you have to sit through in order to get to the cafeteria for lunch? Or, yeah! This is my favorite class! Whether you look forward to science or dread it, you can't escape it. Science is all around us all the time.

What do you think of when you think about science? People in lab coats peering anxiously through microscopes while scribbling notes? Giant telescopes scanning the universe for signs of life? Submersibles trolling the dark, cold, and lonely world of the deepest ocean? Yes, these are all science and things that scientists do to learn more about our planet, outer space, and the human body. But we are all scientists. Even you.

Science is about asking questions. Why do I have to eat my vegetables? Why does the sun set in the west? Why do cats purr and dogs bark? Why am I warmer when I wear a black jacket than when I wear a white one? These are all great questions. And these questions can be the start of something big . . . the start of scientific discovery.

1. **Observe:** Ask questions. What do you see in the world around you that you don't understand? What do you wish you knew more about? Remember, there is always more than one solution to a problem. This is the starting point for scientists—and it can be the starting point for you, too!

Enrique took a slice of bread out of the package and discovered there was mold on it. "Again?" he complained. "This is the second time this all-natural bread I bought turned moldy before I could finish it. I wonder why."

2. **Research:** Find out what you can about the observation you have made. The more information you learn about your observation, the better you will understand which questions really need to be answered.

Enrique researched the term "all-natural" as it applied to his bread. He discovered that it meant that no preservatives were used. Some breads contain preservatives, which are used to "maintain freshness." Enrique wondered if it was the lack of preservatives that was allowing his bread to grow mold.

3. **Predict:** Consider what might happen if you were to design an experiment based on your research. What do you think you would find?

Enrique thought that maybe it was the lack of preservatives in his bread that was causing the mold. He predicted that bread containing preservatives would last longer than "all-natural" breads.

4. **Develop a Hypothesis:** A hypothesis is a possible answer or solution to a scientific problem. Sometimes, they are written as an "if-then" statement. For example, "If I get a good night's sleep, then I will do well on the test tomorrow." This is not a fact; there is no guarantee that the hypothesis is correct. But it is a statement that can be tested with an experiment. And then, if necessary, revised once the experiment has been done.

Enrique thinks that he knows what is going on. He figures that the preservatives in the bread are what keeps it from getting moldy. His working hypothesis is, "If bread contains preservatives, it will not grow mold." He is now ready to test his hypothesis.

5. **Design an Experiment:** An experiment is designed to test a hypothesis. It is important when designing an experiment to look at all the variables. Variables are the factors that will change in the experiment. Some variables will be independent—these won't change. Others are dependent and will change as the experiment progresses. A control is necessary, too. This is a constant throughout the experiment against which results can be compared.

Enrique plans his experiment. He chooses two slices of his bread, and two slices of the bread with preservatives. He uses a small kitchen scale to ensure that the slices are approximately the same weight. He places a slice of each on the windowsill where they will receive the same amount of sunlight. He places the other two slices in a dark cupboard. He checks on his bread every day for a week. He finds that his bread gets mold in both places while the bread with preservatives starts to grow a little mold in the sunshine but none in the cupboard.

6. **Revise the hypothesis:** Sometimes the result of your experiment will show that the original hypothesis is incorrect. That is okay! Science is all about taking risks, making mistakes, and learning from them. Rewriting a hypothesis after examining the data is what this is all about.

Enrique realized it may be more than the preservatives that prevents mold. Keeping the bread out of the sunlight and in a dark place will help preserve it, even without preservatives. He has decided to buy smaller quantities of bread now, and keep it in the cupboard.

This book has activities for you to try at the end of each chapter. They are meant to be fun, and teach you a little bit at the same time. Sometimes, you'll be asked to design your own experiment. Think back to Enrique's experience when you start designing your own. And remember—science is about being curious, being patient, and not being afraid of saying you made a mistake. There are always other experiments to be done!

1
RISING TEMPERATURES

"I don't know why I had to come to this camp," Enzo grumbled to himself as he followed the other campers down the path toward the meeting hall. "I didn't want to come. Mom and dad made me do this."

He was still in a foul mood when the camp director divided the campers into groups and assigned them a counselor. Enzo's group was assigned to Joaquin. Joaquin was enthusiastic and ready to start the day.

"Okay, everyone, here is our first task," said the dark-haired young man. "Here at Enviro-Camp, we are lucky. We get to experience nature and the environment first hand. How often do you get to spend two weeks in the Rocky Mountains?"

Enzo snorted. A girl standing next to him elbowed him in the ribs. "Shh!" she said. "I'm looking forward to this!"

Joaquin continued, "For our first experience, we are going for a walk. Later we will come back here, look at some maps, and do some experiments. Okay, let's go." He took off at a brisk pace out of the campsite.

Enzo turned to the girl next to him. "Why did you poke me?"

"I thought you needed it," she said. "You seemed grumpy. This is going to be fun, you know. I'm Molly. Nice to meet you."

Reluctantly, Enzo shook her outstretched hand. "Enzo," he said. "And I'm not so sure. My parents shipped me off to this camp because they think I needed to get out of the city for a few weeks. I would much rather be at home skateboarding with my friends."

Words to Understand

ecosystem community of living organisms and nonliving things that are found in a specific area

global warming rise in global temperatures over the past century and its consequences

photosynthesis process by which plants use carbon dioxide and energy from the sun to create energy and release oxygen

The two of them followed Joaquin and the other campers in their group. "Oh, come on." Molly said. "Give it a chance. I've heard great things. I think it will be an adventure."

"Yeah, an adventure in mosquito bites," Enzo grumbled, slapping at the insect that landed on his arm.

Joaquin stopped about a mile from camp in a grove of trees. "Look around you. What do you see?"

"Trees," someone answered. The group giggled nervously.

"Yes, trees. But what is it about these trees?" he asked. "Take a close look at them. Go ahead, walk around, touch them. Examine the bark, the roots, the forest floor. Spend some time out there and let's gather back here in a bit."

The campers wandered through the forest. Molly and Enzo walked together. "I think these trees are dead," Molly said, looking up at the branches overhead.

"Gee, you think?" Enzo said sarcastically, looking up at the grey branches lacking leaves. He stopped. "Listen. I don't hear any birds, either."

"You're right," Molly said. "It's as if the whole forest is dead."

Enzo and Molly walked around and looked more carefully at the trees. The darkened trees showed evidence of a forest fire. There were also marks indicating that insects had eaten away a lot of the bark and other layers of the tree. Molly also noticed that there wasn't much vegetation growing anywhere in the area. The ground was packed hard, not soft and spongy as the woods had been closer to the camp.

Once Joaquin got the campers back into their group he began to ask questions. "What do you think happened here?"

"It looks as if there was a forest fire," replied one camper.

Enzo spoke up, "Yeah, but I thought forest fires can be a good thing for a forest. You know, the idea of a fire clearing out the dead brush to make room for the new growth and adding nutrients to the soil. I thought those were good things."

"I'm impressed, Enzo. You know a lot about forest fires," said Joaquin. "Yes, under normal circumstances, a forest fire can be very healthy to a forest **ecosystem**. But something else is going on here."

"You know, I saw a lot of insects hopping around the trees, too," another camper said.

Joaquin nodded. "Scientists have studied these woods for about a decade and found some alarming things. Yes, there are a lot of insects here. Many of these are insects that can harm, not help, the trees. There have been three major fires here in the past twenty years. That's a lot. And many of these signs point to **global warming** as a cause."

Molly raised her hand. "Global warming? As in ice sheets melting? How is that affecting our trees here?"

Joaquin held up his hand. "That's not even the biggest question. The bigger question is how does this forest here impact the rest of the world?"

The group of students seemed skeptical at this question.

Joaquin smiled and went on. "Not that I want to teach you science or anything, but does everyone remember what happens during **photosynthesis**?"

"I know!" a camper chimed in. "Plants take carbon dioxide out of the air and then use energy from the sun to convert the carbon dioxide to oxygen and energy."

Global Warming or Climate Change?

Some are skeptical of the idea of global warming. Scientists point out that it should be called climate change, since warming is only part of the issue. Disbelievers point to the fact that extreme cold snaps and huge winter storms batter parts of the country and the world during the winter months. However, scientists explain that colder than usual temperatures and severe winter storms are indeed part of climate change. A phenomenon called Arctic Oscillation is the mix of the jet stream and air from the Arctic regions. This movement of the jet stream can bring colder-than-usual temperatures to many northern regions around the globe. It can be super cold, even as we warm!

Molly looked thoughtful. "Then without the trees here in this forest, there will be more carbon dioxide in the air."

"And the more carbon dioxide, the warmer the climate," Enzo concluded.

Joaquin smiled again. "This is a simplified, small-scale look at what is happening. Carbon dioxide is a greenhouse gas, responsible for trapping heat close to Earth's surface. Carbon dioxide enters the atmosphere when fossil fuels are burned, or when massive forest fires destroy acres and acres of land. Forest fires mean fewer trees which are used to "clean" the atmosphere of carbon dioxide. It's a vicious cycle."

The group continued their walk in silence, wondering what the future held.

Try It Yourself

Climate change could result in a rapid melting of the polar ice sheets. If the ice sheet over Greenland melted, for example, sea level–across the planet–would rise by an estimated 20 feet (about six meters). If the ice sheet over Antarctica completely melted, sea level would rise 200 feet (about 60 meters)! How much water is really in ice? Try this experiment and find out.

Materials:
- paper cup or liquid measuring cup
- kitchen scale
- ice cubes
- tap water

1. Use the kitchen scale to find the mass of the paper cup or measuring cup.
2. Add water to the cup and find the new mass.
3. Find the mass of 4–5 large ice cubes.
4. Add those to the water.
5. Allow the ice cubes to melt.
6. How much did the mass change? How much water was added to the cup when the ice cubes melted? Was it the same as the amount of water? Or was it more or less?

2
THE POWER OF RECYCLING

"Hey, Enzo!"

Enzo turned as Molly rushed up to him in the cafeteria. "You know," she said, "you shouldn't throw that can in the regular garbage. It can be recycled." She reached into the trash, pulled the can out and then deposited it in the recycle bin next to the trash.

Enzo looked at her as if she had lost her mind. "Seriously? Do you think my one little can is going to make that big of a difference? It's not like I am ruining the Earth single-handedly."

Molly followed him out of the cafeteria. "You sure are grumpy, Enzo. Why is that?"

"And you sure are nosy." He turned to look at her. "Okay, I'm sorry. I just didn't want to come to this camp in the first place. And now there are all these rules and everyone seems to be so into protecting the environment. It's just not something I'm that interested in."

Words to Understand

compost organic material that has been decomposed and used again as fertilizer

emissions gases expelled during natural or artificial processes

landfill site for the disposal of waste materials

Molly nodded and said, "Well, maybe you just haven't had the chance to think about it. Come with me."

Molly and Enzo walked to an area of the camp that was far from the other buildings. There they found Joaquin. He was digging into a large black container with a pitchfork.

"Hi Joaquin," Molly said. "Enzo and I wanted to see if we could help you."

Joaquin stopped digging and stood up. "Great! I could really use some help turning over this **compost**. And there is a new batch that is ready to be spread on the garden over here."

He gave Molly the pitchfork and motioned to Enzo to follow him. Along the way he explained what was happening. "A couple of years ago, I planted a garden here at the camp. I started a composting effort at the same time. We take the food waste from the cafeteria and turn it into useable fertilizer for the garden."

Enzo stared at the soil Joaquin was spreading between the plants. "You mean that is food?"

"Well, not all food. But it is a fair amount of the food waste that is generated in the kitchen. Things like vegetable scraps, eggshells, and the cores or peels from fruits are commonly composted. What most people don't realize is that things like old bread, pretzels, or noodles can be composted, too. Things made out of flour. Coffee grounds, tea bags, spices, and grains can go in there too. You just want to keep things like meat, bones, dairy products, and grease out of the compost. Those things attract animals and maggots and will mess up the nutrients in the compost."

Enzo squatted down so he was close to the compost. "It doesn't even stink. I would have thought that it would really smell like rotting fruit or something."

Joaquin shook his head. "Nope. If it is done right, a compost pile really doesn't smell. Covering it with fresh grass cuttings or hay, burying the fresher waste, and keeping a good flow of air in and out of the pile makes a big difference. That helps keep the fruit flies away, too."

Molly came over to help out. "That's why we have to separate things in the cafeteria, Enzo. I wanted you to see where the stuff was going."

Enzo looked surprised. "Oh, I had no idea. But what about the stuff you can't compost?"

"Well, there are a lot of different options. Most of the other trash items can be recycled. Cans, plastics, paper, all those can be recycled. This leaves a very small amount of actual trash and it helps keep things with other uses out of **landfills**."

"And think about this," Molly said, "I did a research project on recycling last year in school. Twenty recycled cans can be produced with the same amount of energy needed to make only one can from raw materials. And about 80 percent of the glass that makes it into a new glass bottle or jar is recycled glass. So recycling just one glass bottle can make a huge difference!"

"I really didn't know all this. But I am ready to start recycling and composting now," Enzo declared.

Consider This

On average, each person recycles or composts 1.5 pounds (.6 kg) of municipal solid waste each day. This is 1.5 pounds (.6 kg) of waste that does not go to a landfill. But it also saves nearly 3 pounds (1.3 kg) of carbon dioxide **emissions**. The process of manufacturing brand new aluminum cans, glass bottles or cardboard boxes uses energy, which creates carbon dioxide emissions.

Try It Yourself

Spread the word. A lot of people think just what Enzo did—that their personal attempt at recycling won't make that much difference. But, this is simply not true. Try this activity to see how much you can decrease the amount of trash that you put into the landfills.

Materials:
- bag of garbage from household kitchen
- three extra garbage bags
- newspapers
- rubber gloves
- bathroom scale

1. Weigh the garbage bag on a bathroom scale.
2. Spread the newspapers on the floor or on a table. Open the garbage bag and empty the contents on the papers.
3. Put on the rubber gloves and begin to pick through the garbage. Sort it into three piles—items that can be recycled, items that could be composted, and items that are truly trash.
4. Continue until all is sorted. Add each of the three piles to a clean garbage bag and weigh each of them.
5. Which pile was the largest? What percentage of the original trash bag did that occupy? How small was your actual trash? How much did you keep out of landfills?
6. Find appropriate places to recycle and/or compost your waste. And keep up the good work!

3
CLEAN WATER

Joaquin took his group of campers on another hike later in the week. He had a spot in mind that he wanted them to see.

"Here we are. Go ahead and take your backpacks off and take a break. We are going to be taking some water samples in a little bit."

Molly flung herself and her backpack to the ground. "Phew," she sighed, "that was a long hike. I wonder why we had to come all the way out here."

Enzo flopped down beside her. "I don't know. Sure is peaceful out here, though."

Molly grinned. "See, you are starting to get the hang of this thing after all."

Joaquin called the group together. He took some photographs out of his pack and passed them around. "This is what this area looked like a decade ago."

The photograph showed a much different pond. There was very little vegetation around the edges. The water looked dirty and sludgy. "Wow," Molly said, "what happened?"

Joaquin handed each of the students a **vial** in which to put a water sample. "The **acidification** of the pond. That's what happened."

"What does that mean?" the campers wanted to know.

"The water in this pond had at that time acid levels measuring around 5. This was enough to impact the life around the pond in a very negative way."

Enzo raised his hand. "I forget what that means. I know I learned it in science class this year, but what does the 5 mean?"

Words to Understand

acidification a decrease in the pH level of a body of water

fossil fuels substances created by long-term decay of organic material; fossil fuels include oil and natural gas

pH scale used to measure how basic or acidic an aqueous solution is

precipitation water that falls from the sky as snow, rain, hail, or sleet

runoff water that flows off land into bodies of water

vial a small tube, usually with a stopper

Joaquin nodded. "I know, it's hard to think about school stuff during the summer! Liquids can be compared on a scale of pH. That basically stands for the power of hydrogen, an important element that is in most liquids. The **pH scale** ranges from 0 to 12. Something with a pH of 0 is extremely acidic. In fact, anything below a pH of 7 is considered to be acidic. Things with a pH above 7 are basic. Lye and ammonia are basic. Battery acid, lemon juice, soda, and vinegar are all acidic. That means that a safe pH number is in a very small range, about 6 or so."

Molly looked around at the area surrounding the stream. "How did the water in this pond become acidic? I don't see anything that could have leaked acid into the water."

"Well, it wasn't really a leak," Joaquin began. "It was more of a shower."

"Acid rain!" one of the campers shouted.

"Yes. Acid rain. Acid snow, sleet, and hail. It's known as acid **precipitation**. That's the cause of the acidity of the water.

"Acid rain results from a chemical reaction. Compounds like sulfur dioxide and nitrogen oxide enter into the air. Some of the compounds are the result of natural processes like volcanic eruptions or vegetation that has decayed. But much of it comes from our actions—primarily the production of electricity. The power plants that generate electricity often use **fossil fuels** like coal. Burning coal releases these compounds in the air. Car exhaust also releases sulfuric acid and nitrogen oxide into the air. These compounds enter the atmosphere and fall back to earth with the precipitation."

Acidification of the Oceans

It's not just bodies of freshwater that are affected by acid precipitation and **runoff**. There is an ongoing decrease in the pH of Earth's oceans. This is called ocean acidification. Scientists estimate that roughly 35 percent of the carbon dioxide humans release into the atmosphere from burning fossil fuels

and other practices ends up in a dissolved form in the oceans, rivers, and lakes. Studies show that from 1751 to 1994 the pH of the surface water in the oceans decreased from 8.25 to 8.14. That might not seem like a lot to you, but to the organisms living in the ocean that makes a very big difference.

Enzo caught on. "And that rain then falls into the streams and ponds and on the ground, and that contaminates things."

"Yes, you are right."

Molly was confused. "Then why is the pond cleaner now? What happened?"

"Good observation. That's actually a very positive thing here. As the factories in the cities started to switch from coal to other cleaner forms of fuel, the rates of acid rain started to decrease. Slowly, over time, the water quality improved to the state that it's in today."

"That's pretty impressive," Molly admitted.

"But," Joaquin warned, "this pond is pretty small. It's a lot easier to clean things up on a small scale like this. Larger rivers, lakes, and the oceans are polluted, too. It will take a much bigger effort to clean those up."

Try It Yourself!

What does acid rain do to plants? Try this experiment to find out!

Materials:
- two cuttings from a flowering plant
- two cuttings from a fern
- vinegar
- measuring cups and spoons
- pH strips (check with your pharmacy or chemistry teacher)
- baking soda

1. Make an acidic solution by adding one teaspoon of vinegar to two cups of distilled water. The pH of this solution should be about 4. If it is lower than that, add a sprinkling of baking soda. If it is above 4, add a few drops of vinegar until the pH is approximately 4.

2. Measure the pH of distilled water. It should be around 7. If it is above 7, add a drop of vinegar. If it is below 7, add a small amount of baking soda. Adjust as needed until the pH is 7.

3. Label the jars as follows: water & fern, acid & fern, water & flowering plant, acid & flowering plant.

4. Add one cup of water or acid to each of the appropriate jars. Add the plant to the jars a well.

5. Leave plants undisturbed near sunlight for two weeks.

6. Check every two days to make sure the water has not evaporated. Make new solutions as needed.

7. After one week, compare the growth of new roots in each plant.

8. Check again after two weeks. What did you find?

4
CORAL REEFS

Joaquin looked out the window. "Well, you guys, looks like we need to change our plans today. I was hoping to show you the effects of **deforestation**. Instead, I think we are stuck inside." As if to emphasize his statement, a large clap of thunder shook the room. Campers looked up at the ceiling hoping that the roof would hold up against the rain.

"Actually," Joaquin continued once it quieted down a bit, "this is a good thing. I really wanted to talk to you about coral reefs, and of course, we don't really have much of one here."

"What do you mean not much of one? Are you saying we have any coral reefs here in the mountains?" Molly wanted to know.

"Wait, I know," said Enzo, who was starting to get into all this environment talk. "Look at the fish tank!"

"Exactly," said Joaquin. "We have a saltwater fish tank here that has a mini coral reef. Let's go take a closer look at that."

Crowded around the tank, the campers saw different corals and fish. "Now, keep in mind that this is a very controlled environment—and a very small scale. What do you notice about this?" Joaquin left the campers on their own for a bit while they explored.

Molly noticed that certain fish seemed to be hiding in among the corals. "They seem to be hiding in there," she said, pointing them out to the group. "They are not really eating, but hiding."

Another camper pointed at the coral. "These almost look alive. Look how they are moving in the water."

"Well, they are alive," said Joaquin. "Corals are actually animals, not plants."

"And," someone else piped in, "I think there is a **current** being created with that machine right there."

"Look at that thermometer. This water is pretty warm," Molly noticed.

"It says 29°C. That's something like 84°F. It sure is pretty warm," Enzo added.

"Look carefully at the coral. Do they seem to be moving?" Joaquin challenged the campers to take a closer look.

"Well," Enzo observed hesitantly. "They seem to be waving in the current created there. But this one here," he said, pointing to a tube-like projection coming out of the top of one of the corals, "it looks like it is taking food right out of the water."

Joaquin leaned in for a closer look. "Many corals are **filter feeders**. They filter the water through their bodies, taking the microscopic plants out as nutrients. That's what this one's doing now."

One camper had once gone snorkeling on a coral reef off the coast of a Caribbean island. "These ecosystems were amazing. There was so much going on and they look so stable and big."

Joaquin agreed but cautioned the campers. "That's true but these are very fragile ecosystems. Slight changes, such as in temperature or water clarity, or the introduction of contaminants, can have a big impact on the coral reef. Many reefs are dead or dying. We are losing a valuable resource.

"People who live near these areas, along with the govern-

Words to Understand

current flow of water in a lake, stream, ocean or other body of water

deforestation removal of the trees in a forest for reasons other than planting another forest

filter feeder group of animals that eat by straining nutrients from the water

Helpful Reefs

Coral reefs are not just beautiful places that are home to nearly 25 percent of sea life. They play other roles in nature and in our lives. Coral reefs protect shorelines from large waves. This helps cut down on beach erosion. Coral reefs provide food not only to the fish and other sea creatures in the ocean but also to humans. Some drugs and medications used to treat cancer and other diseases are harvested from the organisms in coral reefs. Coral reefs also play an important role in the carbon cycle. This helps maintain a healthy balance of carbon dioxide in the atmosphere—protecting us all.

of contaminants, can have a big impact on the coral reef. Many reefs are dead or dying. We are losing a valuable resource.

"People who live near these areas, along with the governments of those places, are trying to help, but it will take more than a few laws. The other hard part is that this has been going on for a long time, and it will take at least that long to reverse the damage."

"Well," said Enzo. "It's sure worth a try!"

Try It Yourself!

Research time! The goal in this activity is to track all the major coral reefs in the world. On a printout of a world map, mark as many as you can find. Look online, too, for a map showing what area some of the reefs used to cover. Have they expanded . . . or shrunk? Then dig a little deeper. What conservation efforts are being undertaken in Australia or in the Caribbean? What other ideas can you come up with that might help those efforts?

Suggested Materials:
- pen or pencil
- paper
- printed world map

1. Go online and start your search.

2. Try to find as many major coral reef areas as you can.

3. Draw them onto your map; have fun . . . use lots of colors!

4. See if you can find reefs on all of the continents (except Antarctica).

5. Now search for historical maps. What do they show about the change in the size of the reefs?

Bonus: Find three conservation efforts regarding coral reefs. What do they have in common? In what ways are they different?

5
DEFORESTATION

"Take a look at the view from up here," Joaquin encouraged, as the campers finished their climb up the high hill. He spread his arms and proclaimed, "You can see for miles."

Enzo and Molly were in the middle of the pack on the way up. Out of breath, they sat down as soon as they arrived on top of the hill.

"You know," Molly began after she caught her breath, "you can see for miles. But it is kind of weird. It's almost like something is missing up here. There's nothing here."

"Aha!" Joaquin shouted excitedly. "That's what I was looking for! Yes, there is something missing. Who can figure it out?"

The campers looked around. Finally one of them spoke up. "I'm not sure," she said hesitantly. "But I think the trees are missing."

"Exactly. Nothing to be shy about. You are correct. This entire area was clear-cut back in the 1970s. The trees are gone.

"Have you heard of deforestation? This was a case of deforestation on a small scale."

Words to Understand

biodiversity a measurement of the variety of living things

erosion the movement of weathered material

rainforest one of Earth's biomes; characterized by warm temperatures and high yearly rainfall rates

"So what happened?" asked Enzo. "I know that deforestation is done in the Amazon **rainforest** to clear the forest for farming or for building. What happened here?"

"The entire hillside was clear-cut for its lumber and for future development," said Joaquin. "That future development didn't happen. Now we are left with a hill with very few trees.

"But, I'd like you to think of what might have happened back then, right after the trees were cut down. I'd like you to spend some time exploring the area and report back on the effects you find."

The campers split into small groups to explore the hillside. They examined the hillside, the soil, the plants, and nearby streams. Talking among themselves, they all came up with a few observations to report back to the group with.

As the group sat and ate their lunches an hour later, Joaquin asked them what they had found.

"We noticed that the soil was pretty thin on parts of the hill," one group reported. "We aren't sure, but we think that this is the result of an increase in **erosion**."

"Oh? Interesting. Tell me why you think that," encouraged Joaquin.

"Well, with no trees or roots or anything to hold the soil in place, it seems as if the soil would move easily downhill. You know, when it rains or in the spring when the snow melts."

"And you are exactly right!" Joaquin said enthusiastically. "Great job. What else did you find?"

Enzo raised his hand. "I saw all those things, too. But I think there are other impacts of deforestation that we really can't see here in this forest, aren't there?"

Joaquin clapped his hands. "Absolutely. The impact of deforestation is great, and sometimes we can't even see it. For example, there is the concern about loss of **biodiversity**. When the trees are cut down there are more organisms impacted than just the trees. Birds, reptiles, mammals, and other plants are hurt by this. The animals may die or have to move to other areas. The variety of life here in this area is impacted."

The campers all looked around, as if trying to see what animals were left.

"Okay, what else could happen if a forest is cleared?" Joaquin asked the campers.

"Well, what about photosynthesis?" asked Molly. "If we cut down the trees, then there is not as much carbon dioxide removed from the atmosphere. Could that have an impact?"

Joaquin nodded slowly. "Yes. And that is one of the concerns. Think about this. Some scientists think that as much as 80,000 acres of tropical rainforest are lost—each day! That is a staggering number of trees that are not removing carbon dioxide from the atmosphere. The effect on the Earth's climate is huge."

"What happens to those 80,000 acres that are cleared?" asked Enzo. "I mean, why is this happening?"

"The majority of the forests are cleared for business reasons. Logging, mining, agriculture, the building of dams, ranching . . . those are all reasons that people are cutting down the rainforests. Large tracts of land are being cleared for development or simply for the firewood. It's alarming to think about, especially considering those tropical rainforests, in areas like the Amazon, are home to an estimated 50 percent of all Earth's species. We are actually destroying their homes, bit by bit."

Tropical Rainforests and Medicines

Rainforests are in your life every day—nearly half of the medication on the shelves at your local pharmacy originated in tropical rainforests. For example, a periwinkle plant found only in the forests of Madagascar (pictured) increased the survival rate of children with leukemia from 20 percent to 80 percent. How-

ever, the forest that was home to the periwinkle has been destroyed by deforestation. Other rainforest plants contain compounds that are used to make medicines to fight malaria, diabetes, bronchitis, heart disease, and glaucoma. Other medicines and treatments such as antibiotics, laxatives, and anesthetics are made from rainforest plants. Suddenly, these ecosystems don't seem so far away, do they?

Try it Yourself!

One of the immediate concerns about deforestation is the increase in erosion and the resulting removal of topsoil. Try this short activity to see how quickly topsoil is removed when there is no vegetation holding it in place.

Materials:
- large rectangular plastic box
- soil
- a strip of sod (grass covered soil)
- watering can or hose with a sprayer
- several large books

1. Place the soil in the plastic box. Place the sod and grass on top of the soil.

2. Raise one end of the box with the books.

3. Use the watering can to replicate rain falling on the soil. Pour the water on the raised end of the box. Really drench it, as if it were a quick downpour. What happens when the rain falls on the sod and grass? Describe what you see. Check closely at the lower end of the box.

4. Now carefully remove the sod and grass, exposing the topsoil beneath.

5. Again, create a "rainstorm" over the raised end of the box.

6. What happens? Look closely at the lower end of the box. What do you see there?

6

THE IMPACT OF MINING

An announcement came over the camp's PA system. "Will Joaquin's group please meet out by the vans after breakfast? Bring your backpacks with notebooks and pencils. Pick up your bagged lunch before you leave."

"Where do you think we are going?" Molly asked when she met Enzo near the tables covered with bags of lunches.

"Not sure. But with Joaquin, you can bet it will involve some sort of physical activity."

Once on the bus, Joaquin had an exercise for the campers to complete. "Okay, I want you to make a list of all the things you have used today. Everything. I'll give you five minutes. Ready, set, go!"

Joaquin set the timer on his watch while he watched the campers scribble in their notebooks.

"Time's up. Pencils down. What do we have?"

The campers started to call out their items while Joaquin wrote them into different columns on the white board: toothpaste . . . toast . . . shampoo . . . cell phone . . . razor . . . radio . . . sneakers . . . Twinkies.

"Twinkies?" Joaquin stopped for a second while the other campers giggled. "Who's eating Twinkies at eight in the morning?"

One of the campers sheepishly raised her hand. "It was the last one my mom sent in my care package."

"I see. And for those of you

Words to Understand

groundwater water that is held in underground springs to be used by people

mine place where valuable minerals and ores are extracted from the earth

open-pit mine surface-mining technique where minerals are removed from ground by removing layers of soil in an open pit

veins long, thin seams or layers of minerals inside a larger area of rock

who said you used your cell phone at times other than the camp says are okay . . . I'll forget that. But what we have here is a very interesting list. And it looks like we have arrived at our destination."

The campers looked out the windows at a dusty, barren hole in the ground. Huge dump trucks drove around terraces that had been cut into the sides of the **mine**. From the top of the mine, the trucks looked very small.

Opening the bus door, Joaquin announced, "We are now on the edge of one of the largest mining operations in the area. Stay close to me, and don't wander off."

The campers followed Joaquin into a building near a road headed down into the mine. Inside there were maps, diagrams, and samples of the ore being removed from the ground.

A park ranger came up to the group. "Welcome. I'm here to give you a quick tour of the mine. This is a gold mine. It started in the 1880s, but back then it was mainly an underground mine."

Enzo raised his hand. "You mean, people would go underground to get the gold?"

The ranger nodded. "Yes. The gold was concentrated in **veins** and the miners would pick away at the veins, removing the rock that contained the gold. They eventually made paths through the rock and deep into the ground. Eventually, the miners dug a tunnel more than six miles long."

The ranger pointed to some photographs on the wall. "We started the **open-pit** operation in the 1990s. The price of gold was such that we were able to have a more extensive mining operation to get smaller amounts of the mineral."

The campers and Joaquin looked out the windows from the visitors' center. From there, they could see nothing but terraces of exposed soil and rock. Large trucks rumbled, dust kicked up, and the sun blazed down on the whole scene.

On the bus back to camp, Joaquin asked the students what they thought.

Molly was the first to speak up. "That mine was like a giant scar in the ground. There was nothing else around there. Everything had been removed. It was bleak."

"And we've been talking so much about erosion," added Enzo. "That place must be a nightmare when it rains."

"But at least it is outside," said another camper. "Can you imagine being a miner in a long tunnel in the ground? I would be worried the whole time about not getting back out or about the mine collapsing or something."

Someone else said, "All those trucks and big pieces of equipment are dangerous, too. And the pollution. Did you see how those trucks were sending up clouds of exhaust and stuff?"

Joaquin nodded as the campers spoke. "You are all on the right track. There are many, many environmental concerns when it comes to mining. Contamination of **groundwater**, runoff, the health and safety of the miners, disruption of ecosystems…these are all factors. But consider the fact that they are mining gold. Do you think that is worth the cost to the environment?"

The campers were split on their thoughts. Some felt that the cost of mining was worth the minerals that were removed. Others did not.

"I'd like you to consider this for a minute," said Joaquin. "Look back at those lists you made this morning. Cell phones, razors, even Twinkies. Those are all made of ingredients that are mined out of the ground. Many products, including those tasty snack cakes, contain calcium sulfate, ascorbic acid, and polysorbate 60. These materials are mined from the ground or are petroleum products. The same ingredients are found in sheetrock, jet fuel, and in shampoo."

"But more importantly, many of the things we use every day came from a mine similar to the one we just saw. The impact that these mining operations have on the environment is significant. That's something to consider whenever you use mineral-based products."

Titanium Dioxide

A mineral called rutile, or titanium dioxide, is found in many products that you eat and use. Check the ingredients list on many foods and you'll find titanium dioxide listed. It's found in most red-colored candy and skim milk. It's used in the paint on tennis courts, in cosmetics, and as part of most toothpastes. The largest mines that produce rutile are found in Australia and South Africa, but other countries include Brazil, Ukraine, Mozambique, and India—and that is just one of the many mineral ingredients that come out of the ground . . . and into our lives.

Try It Yourself!

What minerals are in the foods you eat? What's inside the products you use every day? What about the electronics in your home? Spend some time looking at ingredient labels.

Materials:
- any food products that have detailed ingredient lists
- a list (find one online) of the materials used to make a toaster

1. Look carefully at the ingredients in the food and the list of materials in the toaster.

2. Which might be mineral products? Make a list of any you suspect.

3. Research online or in a chemistry textbook to find out which of the chemicals you have on your list are from the ground, and which are not.

4. Did you find any that you cannot figure out? Those might be compounds created from other things from the ground. Dig a little deeper (pardon the pun) to find out.

5. How many ingredients did you come up with? Make a chart to see which appeared on the most types of food. For the most common ones, do more research to find out how much is used in the United States, what are the most common sources, and what alternatives might replace the product?

7
INVASIVE SPECIES

"Wow, look at that crayfish," Enzo called out. "He's really going after the other one over there!" Enzo stood on a rock looking into a small pool of water in part of the stream. The campers had been taking water samples for an experiment they would do later.

"Let me take a look at that," Joaquin said as he clambered over some rocks to see what Enzo was looking at. "Just as I thought. It's a rusty crayfish." He grabbed it by the back and called the rest of the group over to look at it.

"You can tell it's a rusty crayfish by these two rust colored spots on its back," Joaquin said. "We need to take down some notes here so we can alert the authorities. Here, Enzo, hold it right like I am so I can take its picture."

Molly was confused. "Joaquin, why is this necessary? Who do we have to alert?"

The counselor snapped a picture with his cell phone camera and then turned to Molly. "This is an **invasive species** here in this part of the Rocky Mountains. We need to tell the state board of conservation where we found it."

Words to Understand

aquatic living in the water

invasive species a species introduced into an area that is not native

microbes microorganisms that usually produce disease

"An invasive species? What's that?" Molly wanted to know.

Joaquin explained, "An invasive species, or introduced species as they are sometimes called, is a species of plant or animal that is not native to the area. It was brought here some other way. Apparently, the rusty crayfish was used as bait and introduced that way. Some also think that local schools used these crayfish in their laboratory exercises and then released the animals into the wild. That could have helped spread the population."

"But what's the problem?" asked another camper. "Why all the concern? Can the crayfish population really be that big now? What's a few more crayfish?"

"I think I know," piped in Enzo. "It's not just the addition of more crayfish. It's the impact the crayfish will have on the ones that were here first. Isn't that right Joaquin?"

"Good job, Enzo," said Joaquin. "That's exactly right. These crayfish are more aggressive than the native crayfish. They will come into their territory and take it over. These crayfish eat a lot of **aquatic** plants, too, which alters the ecosystem. There are fewer plants then for other organisms to eat and hide in, which upsets the balance. There is some evidence that these rusty crayfish may eat the eggs of the native fish in the stream, which is something the native crayfish don't do. And of course, there is always the chance that the crayfish that are native to this area may catch diseases or bacteria being carried by these invasive crayfish, which could harm them."

Molly stared at the crayfish between Enzo's fingers and let out a low whistle. "Wow. All that from this little thing?"

"Yeah. See why invasive species can be so dangerous to ecosystems?" Joaquin asked.

"But, really, it seems like this is not really that big of a deal. Can one little crayfish really make that much of a difference?" another camper wanted to know.

Joaquin sat on the rock in the stream and held the crayfish. "Well, think of it this way. Species, both plant and animal, are adapted to their own environment. And in turn, the environment and ecosystem around it is adapted to it. An invasive species could prey on local, native species. They often compete with the native species for the same food sources, and sometimes they win. They may introduce new diseases into the ecosystem that they can handle but that native animals or plants can't.

"And they have other impacts, too. They may change the food web in the area and this can lead to a decrease in biodiversity. These invasive species of plants and animals have altered landscapes and ecosystems and harmed the natural vegetation in many areas."

"Wow. Sounds like a sci-fi movie if you ask me," commented Enzo.

Joaquin carefully placed the crayfish back in the water and watched it scuttle away. "Invasive species are no joke. And they aren't things of fiction. People need to be aware of the species that may be clinging to the bottom of their boats. They need to know that shipping pallets may have insects from around the world hiding in them. Ornamental plants may be introduced to the outside and spread. And the exotic pet trade introduces many invasive species into our natural habitats."

"I had no idea," said Enzo. "I guess this crayfish is just a very small example of what can go wrong."

Not Just Plants and Animals

Invasive species can be more than just plants and animals. Certain **microbes** are considered invasive species, too. One of the more well known invasive species in North America right now is the West Nile Virus. This virus, which is passed between animals and to humans by mosquito bites, was first identified in the East African country of Uganda. By 2012, it had spread to much of the United States, Europe, parts of Canada, the Caribbean, and Latin America. The virus killed 84 people in 2014 in the United States alone. Some invasive species can have a devastating impact.

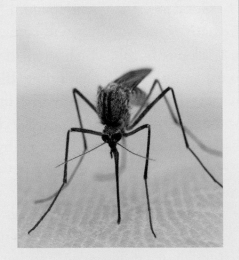

Try It Yourself!

Many of us may come in contact with invasive species on a regular basis and not even know it. Do you, or someone you know, own a boat? Or an exotic pet? Or have tropical house plants? Or take firewood from state to state? Education about invasive species is increasing. Here is your chance to help the environment, and teach your friends and family about the dangers of invasive species.

Materials:
- poster board
- markers, colored pencils
- Internet access

1. Pick an invasive species you'd like to investigate. Invasive species can be brought in intentionally or accidentally. You may want to pick one that is local to your area.

2. Use Internet resources to find out about the particular species you chose. How does it enter an ecosystem? What harm does it do? What can be done about it?

3. Make an educational poster describing the impact the invasive species can have. Add helpful hints to preventing the spread of the species throughout the ecosystem.

8
ENDANGERED SPECIES

On the way back to camp, Joaquin stopped the group under the trees where the soil was damp from the previous rains. "Look at that. That's a great sign."

Molly looked around. "What are you looking at? I can't see anything up there."

"No, down here." Joaquin pointed to the ground. There in the soft soil was a cat's footprint. The campers leaned in closer and could see the outline of the soft pads on the big cat's foot and the indentations from its claws. "These are prints of a Canadian lynx."

Enzo immediately looked up into the trees. "A lynx? Is it stalking us right now?"

Joaquin chuckled and said, "I doubt it. We are a pretty big group for one lynx to take on. The amazing thing is that we are even seeing its footprints now. In the 1970s and 1980s, the lynx was being trapped for its fur. Activists and scientists tried to get the cat on the list of endangered species but the federal government refused to add it to the list. The trouble got even worse in the 1990s when the lynx was further threatened by habitat loss due to logging. It was pretty complicated, but eventually, thanks to the hard work of biologists, and activists, and some government leaders, the Canadian lynx was granted threatened status by the Fish and Wildlife Service in 2000."

Words to Understand

endangered in immediate danger of becoming extinct

threatened in biology, having numbers so low a species as a whole is close to becoming endangered

"What is the difference between an **endangered** species and a **threatened** one?" asked Molly.

"Great question. To put it in basic terms, an endangered species is in real, immediate danger of becoming extinct. Threatened species have population numbers that put them on the brink of being endangered."

"And once a species is extinct, that's it. There's no coming back from extinction," Enzo said.

"Right," Joaquin agreed. "That is why the fact that we are finding these lynx footprints here is a good thing. Having the lynx labeled as a threatened species has obviously helped it. The population must be increasing."

"So the level of danger to an organism can change? For the better?" someone asked.

"Oh, yes. In fact, one of the most amazing and well known success stories is the bald eagle," Joaquin explained. "The bald eagle was put on the list of endangered species in 1973. Habitat loss and pesticide use had reduced its population in the United States. But thanks to conservation efforts and regulations on pesticide use, the status of the bald eagle was upgraded to threatened in 1995. In 2007, it was removed from the list of threatened species completely!"

The bald eagle is an endangered species success story.

"Well, that's good, then." Molly agreed. "I guess there are more successes like that today."

"Sadly, no. There are many more species that are endangered, and many that go extinct. In 1989, a golden toad found in the forests of Costa Rica disappeared forever. A fish called the Tecopa pupfish that lived in hot springs in the Mojave Desert died off in 1982. And the West African black rhino, once found in Cameroon, was declared extinct in 2006. Experts estimate that perhaps one-tenth of one percent of the world's plant or animal species go extinct each year. If there are 100,000,000 species in the world, then that would be at least 10,000 species every year."

The campers were shocked and saddened to learn that.

"I guess extinctions aren't just for the dinosaurs and the woolly mammoths. They are happening right now," said Enzo sadly.

Joaquin put his hand on Enzo's shoulder as the group continued back to camp. "Sometimes extinction is a natural thing, just the cycle of life. Unfortunately, sometimes human actions can speed up the whole process."

It's Plants, Too!

Many of us tend to think of animals when we think about endangered or threatened species. Plant species are at just as much risk, if not more so in some cases. For example, estimates put the total population of the western  prairie fringed orchid (pictured) at fewer than 1,000 plants. They are only found in five U.S. states and are harmed by rising temperatures, prairie fires, and development. The Wiggin's acalypha is found only on the Galapagos Islands and is disappearing due to habitat loss. This plant is considered to be critically endangered. The *stenogyne kanehoana*, a member of the mint family, was thought to be extinct until a single plant was found in Hawaii.

Try It Yourself!

Plants and animals become extinct for many reasons. How many of those reasons can be tied directly to human activities? Do some research and find out.

Suggested Materials:
- Internet access
- paper
- pencil

1. Pick one plant and one animal species that have become extinct in recent years.

2. Research the history of the animal and find out all you can about it: what did it eat, where did it live, what were its habits?

3. Find out when it was last seen and where.

4. What do scientists say were the reasons it disappeared? Did people try to save it or not?

5. Repeat the process for the plant species.

6. What common reasons can you find between the two extinctions? What might have been done to prevent them from happening?

For a bonus activity: Find a very endangered animal species and research what is being done to help it. Can you think of other ways that might help prevent it from becoming extinct, too?

9
CONCLUSION

Environmental Science. As the campers at EnviroCamp learned, there are so many things that fall under the umbrella of environmental science. Basically, just about anything that has to do with the world around us can be considered environmental science.

Some branches of environmental science deal with the health and status of organisms around the world. Studies looking at the rate of extinctions of species, the issues surrounding habitat loss, changes to habitats due to climate change, the invasion of nonnative species—these are all concerns of environmental scientists. It's important to remember, however, that the organisms we are concerned with include more than the cute animals we see on the news. Giant pandas, the Sumatran tiger, and the mountain gorilla are all endangered or critically endangered. They have been seen in TV specials and in long magazine articles. People raise money around the world to help save those well known creatures . . . and that's a good thing. But there are other organisms—including plants—that need our help to ensure their survival.

Environmental science looks at human-caused problems as well. As Molly and Enzo found out, the impact of mining, global climate change, and deforestation have significant and long lasting effects on the environment. Educating people and pushing to change our overall behavior and ways we think about Earth and our role here is necessary to keep our planet healthy.

That can start with each individual person. There are personal choices we all can make to reduce our impact on the environment, such as recycling, making wise choices of the foods we eat and the products we buy, and being aware of our carbon footprint. These are all things we can do.

You can make a difference, too. Try this. Find an online resource that calculates your personal carbon footprint. A carbon footprint measures your personal impact on the planet in terms of the amount of carbon dioxide you produce. That's not just the air you breathe out. How often do you drive? What fuels do you burn to heat your house? How much electricity do you use every day? All of those, at some point in their processes, produce some level of carbon dioxide. A person's carbon footprint adds up all those amounts to arrive at a number that can be compared to others in a region or a country.

Your carbon footprint is increased by the amount of driving you do.

The U.S. Environmental Protection Agency as well as the World Wildlife Fund have online calculators that are easy to use. Find out how much impact you have on the environment every day. Then make a pledge. Commit to reducing your own personal impact—it might not be as difficult as you think. Then get your friends and family and classmates on board. If we all make small changes, then the results will be huge! You'll get another benefit, too. You'll feel better about your place in the world.

People working together, even on small projects like a beach clean-up, can have a big impact on the health of our planet.

Environmental Science 24-7: Concept Review

Chapter 1
Global warming and climate change aren't just topics that are talked about in science classes and government panels. As Molly and Enzo discovered, there are examples of the impact of these changes all around.

Chapter 2
Small changes in habits can make big differences to the environment. This chapter looked at some of the impacts recycling can have on ecosystems.

Chapter 3
Molly and Enzo discovered that bodies of water can be healthy, or not, and that sometimes the cause of pollution can be very far away.

Chapter 4
Coral reefs are some of the most vital—and fragile—ecosystems in the world, as this chapter explained.

Chapter 5
Imagine a forest with no trees. Sounds crazy, doesn't it? In this chapter, Molly and Enzo learn that forests around the world are being cut down.

Chapter 6
Think about all you use in a day. Most of it, including the food you eat, the computers you use, and the vehicles you ride around in, had to be mined out of the ground.

Chapter 7
Some houseguests arrive unannounced and overstay their welcome. Invasive species are often like these guests—but with a far more serious impact.

Chapter 8
You've probably heard that nothing lasts forever. But when you are talking about species of animals and plants, the loss of species can be very serious.

Index